Copyright © 2021-All rights reserved.

No part of this publication may be reproduced, distributed, or transmitted in any form or by any means, including photocopying, recording, or other electronic or mechanical methods, without the prior written permission of the publisher, except in the case of brief quotations embodied in reviews and certain other non-commercial uses permitted by copyright law.

This Book is provided with the sole purpose of providing relevant information on a specific topic for which every reasonable effort has been made to ensure that it is both accurate and reasonable. Nevertheless, by purchasing this Book you consent to the fact that the author, as well as the publisher, are in no way experts on the topics contained herein, regardless of any claims as such that may be made within. It is recommended that you always consult a professional prior to undertaking any of the advice or techniques discussed with in.This is a legally binding declaration that is considered both valid and fair by both the Committee of Publishers Association and the American Bar Association and should be considered as legally binding within the United States.

CONTENTS

INTRODUCTION

There is a wide range of toaster ovens available in the market today. Invented by scientist William S. Hadaway in 1910, these small countertop appliances are miniature hybrids of regular toasters and ovens. Instead of gas, toaster ovens run on electricity. They usually come with a removable wire rack and baking tray.

The earlier standard countertop models come in handy for browning, toasting, and reheating different foods. In recent years, the most popular toaster ovens are the convection types with lower energy consumption and carbon footprint compared to other types.

What is BLACK+DECKER Toaster Oven?

The BLACK+DECKER Toaster Oven features a more spacious cooking interior as compared to other convection toaster ovens. The internal dimensions are 16.5 x 12.5 x 9.5 inches and can fit most baking pans with handles that measure 9 x 13 inches. It can accommodate the cooking load of your large standard oven. To illustrate, you can cook a 12-inch pizza or eight (8) slices of bread at once with the BLACK+DECKER Toaster Oven.

This 1,500-watt kitchen gadget has a maximum temperature of 450 degrees F.

How Does It Work?

The BLACK+DECKER Toaster Oven uses advanced convection technology. Its powerful built-in fan circulates hot air inside the oven, which allows the food to cook faster at a lower temperature. This technology also gives evenly cooked results when baking.

This kitchen device uses advanced heating elements, which makes the actual temperature in the oven always lower than the set temperature. But no need to worry about doing your math! Because the dial settings have undergone proper calibration to take these differences in temperatures into account.

Various Functions

The BLACK+DECKER Toaster Oven features four functions: toast, bake, broil, and keep warm. The unit has three rack positions for more flexibility in cooking with different function settings.

To start the toaster oven, turn the control knob to the desired cooking function and then set the unit to the required time. The power indicator light remains on until the timer is done.

Equipped with a dedicated precision toast timer, the BLACK+DECKER Toaster Oven prides on coming up with perfect toast and predictable shade selection every time. You may control the toasting time to Light, Medium, or Dark settings, depending on your preference.

The device comes with a toasting rack. There is also an external crumb tray that you can slide in and out for easy cleaning.

When baking and broiling, always preheat at the required temperature for 10 minutes.

For extended baking requirements, the BLACK+DECKER Toaster Oven has a 60-minute precision timer that features a stay-on function.

When set to broiling, the heating elements at the bottom will be off. That means the unit will generate heat from the top heating elements only. This setting is ideal for cooking vegetables in thin slices, melting cheese, making s'mores, or roasting peppers.

The unit also comes with a baking and broiling pan.

Tips

Always use broiler- and oven-safe pans with the BLACK+DECKER Toaster Oven. If you want to use pans other than those that come with the unit, go for ones with low sides to aid in the convection process by leaving enough room for the hot air to circulate inside the oven.

Take time to find the perfect rack height for your desired cooking results when using a particular function or setting. The middle rack placement may be the safest place, but it does not always give the best results.

When broiling, for instance, using the top rack placement is recommended. But if you end up with burnt food, then you might need to lower the rack position.

When using two or three racks at the same time, rotating and swapping the position of the pans throughout the cooking duration will help get evenly done results.

Also, when broiling, you may need to flip the food to brown on both sides since only the top heating elements are working in this setting.

Matters That Need Attention

Note that the BLACK+DECKER Toaster Oven cooks food fast. You may want to keep an eye on your meal, especially when cooking it for the first time. Adjust to a lower temperature accordingly if you need to be away with another task while cooking to avoid burning the food.

Even with its spacious interior, the BLACK+DECKER Toaster Oven is still more suitable for smaller dishes. If you overcrowd your oven, you may get unevenly cooked results.

Cleaning & Maintenance

As with any other kitchen appliances, regularly cleaning the BLACK+DECKER Toaster Oven is the best way to keep your unit in proper operating conditions. If you neglect yours for too long, the time will come when the best option will be buying a newer model.

Of course, we want you to enjoy and make the most of your appliance for a long time. That is why we recommend that you clean the device after each use. Make sure to unplug it and let it cool down before attempting to touch, clean, or put it away for storage.

Wipe the glass door and outer surface of the toaster oven with a damp washcloth, as necessary. Dry thoroughly.

For the interior, avoid getting the heating elements wet. It is also best to use a homemade solution to clean the inside of the oven safely. Use a moist sponge or washcloth with a mixture of dish soap, vinegar, and warm water.

Remove the crumb tray by sliding it out, and then dispose of the food debris. Build up from grease and food crumbs can cause smoke—or even a fire.

Also, take out the metal rack and tray. Clean these removable components using a sponge or washcloth and a soapy water mixture.

For stubborn stains or stuck-on food, you can soak them overnight. Do not use metal or other abrasive cleaners.

Never submerge the unit itself, including the power cord, in water.

Cooking Timetable

Later, you will find a collection of quick and easy recipes that you can make with the BLACK+DECKER Toaster Oven. But if you have favorite oven-cooked recipes, you can easily convert their cooking times and prepare them using your BLACK+DECKER Toaster Oven.

In general, food cooks up to 30 percent faster in a convection oven than in a regular one. That means the dish needs to be in your toaster oven for 70 percent of the time, instead of 100 percent of the time a standard oven recipe would require.

To illustrate, the standard oven recipe for chicken legs calls for 60 minutes at 300 degrees F. Multiplying 60 minutes by 70 percent (60 times 0.70) will mean you will need 42 minutes only to cook the same recipe in your BLACK+DECKER Toaster Oven.

Another option would be to adjust the temperature instead of the cooking time. That is the better option, especially when dealing with recipes that require shorter cooking times or under 15 minutes. A good ballpark figure is decreasing the cooking temperature by 25 degrees.

Some foods naturally require shorter cooking times. When cooked in a convection oven, they may burn quickly. Lowering the temperature in this case, also prevents a dinner fiasco.

CHAPTER 1: 10 BRUNCH RECIPES

Breakfast Sandwich

Stacked avocado, tomato and cheese on top of English muffin—the breakfast you'd love to have each day.

Prep Time and Cooking Time: 10 minutes | Serves:1

Ingredients to Use:

1 English muffin, split into 2

1 fried egg

1 slice cheese

4 slices avocado

Salt and pepper to taste

Step-by-Step Directions

1. Stack the egg, cheese and avocado on top of the muffin slice.
2. Season with salt and pepper.
3. Top with the other muffin slice.
4. Place inside the toaster oven.
5. Select toast setting.
6. Toast for one cycle.

Serving Suggestion: Sprinkle with sesame seeds.

Tip: Toast for another cycle if not fully done.

Banana Bread

Start your day right with this banana bread breakfast that serves up to 10.

Prep Time and Cooking Time: 45 minutes | Serves:10

Ingredients to Use:

Cooking spray

Dry

1 ½ cups flour

½ cup sugar

1 teaspoon baking soda

¼ teaspoon salt

Wet

1 cup over ripe banana, mashed

1 egg

¼ cup coconut oil

½ cup buttermilk

½ teaspoon vanilla extract

Step-by-Step Directions

1. Preheat your toaster to 325 degrees F.

2. Set it to bake function.

3. Spray your loaf pan with oil.

4. In a bowl, mix the dry ingredients.

5. Add the wet ingredients to another bowl.

6. Pour the wet ingredients to the first bowl.

7. Stir well.

8. Pour the batter into the loaf pan.

9. Bake in the oven for 50 minutes.

Serving Suggestion: Let cool before slicing and serving.

Tip: Use whole-wheat flour and organic pure cane sugar if available.

Baked Oatmeal

A quick and easy breakfast dish that you can prepare even when you're running late.

Prep Time and Cooking Time: 45 minutes | Serves:2

Ingredients to Use:

1/4 cup mashed ripe banana

2 teaspoons olive oil

2 teaspoons maple syrup

1 tablespoon flax meal

1/4 teaspoon baking powder

1/2 teaspoon vanilla extract

1 cup rolled oats

1/2 teaspoon ground cinnamon

1/2 cup almond milk

1/8 teaspoon salt

1/4cup pecans

Step-by-Step Directions

1. Preheat your oven to 350 degrees F.

2. Select bake setting.

3. Grease your toaster oven baking pan.

4. In a bowl, combine mashed banana and the rest of the ingredients.

5. Pour into the baking pan.

6. Bake for 30 minutes.

Serving Suggestion: Garnish with banana slices.

Tip: Store in the refrigerator for up to 3 days. You can also freeze for up to 3 months.

Cornbread Zucchini Muffin

Soft muffins with sweet and savory flavor that you'd enjoy with every bite.

Prep Time and Cooking Time: 30 minutes | Serves:6

Ingredients to Use:

Cooking spray

1 zucchini squash, grated

½ cup yellow cornmeal

½ cup flour

1 tablespoon sugar

1 teaspoon baking powder

1/8 teaspoon baking soda

1 egg, beaten

¼ cup whole milk

¼ cup yogurt

2 tablespoons butter, melted

¼ cup corn kernels

Salt to taste

Step-by-Step Directions

1. Preheat your toaster oven to 350 degrees F.

2. Choose bake setting.

3. Spray your muffin pan with oil.

4. Combine all the ingredients in a bowl.

5. Pour the mixture into the muffin cups.

6. Bake in the toaster oven for 15 minutes.

Serving Suggestion: Let cool for 3 minutes before removing from the muffin pan.

Tip: If you want heartier crumb, skip the yogurt.

Baked Eggs with Green Beans

Serve this filling egg breakfast dish with steamed beans and bread.

Prep Time and Cooking Time: 20 minutes | Serves:2

Ingredients to Use:

8 oz. green beans

½ teaspoon olive oil

Salt and pepper to taste

2 eggs

2 tablespoons half and half

4 tablespoons Parmesan cheese, grated

2 slices whole grain bread

Step-by-Step Directions

1. Preheat your toaster oven to 425 degrees F.

2. Select bake setting.

3. Add the beans to a baking pan.

4. Toss in oil, salt and pepper.

5. Add half and half to the ramekins.

6. Sprinkle with cheese.

7. Crack the eggs in ramekins.

8. Season with salt and pepper.

9. Place the baking pan and ramekin inside the toaster oven.

10. Cook for 6 to 8 minutes.

11. Serve the baked eggs and green beans with the bread slices.

Serving Suggestion: Garnish with chopped chives.

Tip: Bake for a few more minutes if you want hard-cooked yolks.

Frittata

This is a great idea if you have left over veggies from last night's dinner.

Prep Time and Cooking Time: 50 minutes | Serves: 2

Ingredients to Use:

2 teaspoons grapeseed oil, divided

1 shallot, chopped

½ cup broccoli florets, chopped

½ cup Brussels sprouts, chopped

2 mushrooms, chopped

4 eggs, beaten

¼ teaspoon dried oregano

1 roasted red pepper, chopped

2 tablespoons feta cheese, crumbled

2 tablespoons half and half

Chopped parsley

Salt and pepper to taste

Step-by-Step Directions

1. Preheat your oven to 400 degrees F.
2. Choose bake function.
3. Grease your baking pan with oil.
4. Mix all the vegetables in a bowl.
5. Transfer to the baking pan.
6. Slice to the toaster oven.
7. Cook for 15 minutes, stirring once.
8. Stir in the rest of the ingredients.
9. Reduce temperature to 375 degrees F.
10. Bake for another 25 minutes.

Serving Suggestion: Sprinkle with chopped parsley.

Tip: You can also use frozen cooked vegetables.

Egg Muffin with Kale & Feta

Wake your taste buds with these amazing egg muffins with feta cheese and kale.

Prep Time and Cooking Time: 30 minutes | Serves:6

Ingredients to Use:

Cooking spray

4 eggs

¼ cup skim milk

¼ cup feta cheese, crumbled

3 oz. kale, chopped

Salt and pepper to taste

Step-by-Step Directions

1. Preheat your oven to 350 degrees F.

2. Turn to bake setting.

3. Grease your muffin pan with oil.

4. In a bowl, beat the eggs and the rest of the ingredients.

5. Pour the mixture into the muffin pan.

6. Bake in the toaster oven for 20 minutes.

Serving Suggestion: Serve muffins either warm or cold.

Tip: Bake until the edges are browned.

Almond Granola

This is a simple granola recipe that you'd enjoy every morning.

Prep Time and Cooking Time: 30 minutes | Serves:2

Ingredients to Use:

1 ¼ cups rolled oats

¼ cup coconut flakes

¼ cup almonds, slivered

3 tablespoons wheat germ

Pinch salt

2 tablespoons coconut oil

2 tablespoons maple syrup

¼ teaspoon almond extract

Step-by-Step Directions

1. Preheat your toaster oven to 325 degrees F.

2. Choose bake setting.

3. In a bowl, combine the rolled oats, coconut flakes, almonds, wheat germ and salt.

4. In another bowl, mix the remaining ingredients.

5. Pour the second bowl into the first one.

6. Spread the mixture into a baking pan.

7. Bake in the toaster oven for 20 minutes, stirring once.

Serving Suggestion: Let cool before serving.

Tip: Use unsweetened coconut flakes. Chia seeds can also be used in place of wheat germ.

Breakfast Fruit Crumble

This is like having dessert in the morning.

Prep Time and Cooking Time: 30 minutes | Serves:2

Ingredients to Use:

Cooking spray

4 teaspoons grapeseed oil

3 tablespoons almond milk

1/8 teaspoon almond extract

2 teaspoons maple syrup

¼ cup whole wheat flour

¼ teaspoon baking powder

Salt to taste

2 tablespoons almonds, slivered

¼ cup cherries, pitted and sliced in half

Step-by-Step Directions

1. Preheat your toaster oven to 350 degrees F.

2. Select bake setting.

3. Grease your ramekins with oil.

4. Combine oil, almond milk, almond extract and maple syrup in a bowl.

5. In another bowl, mix flour, baking powder and salt.

6. Add the first bowl to the second bowl.

7. Pour the mixture into the ramekins.

8. Press on top the almonds and cherries.

9. Slide the ramekins into the toaster oven.

10. Cook for 10 minutes.

Serving Suggestion: Top with yogurt and drizzle with maple syrup.

Tip: You can also use pistachios instead of almonds.

Peach Breakfast Pizza

It only takes less than 15 minutes to prepare this amazing breakfast pizza topped with peaches when you make use of your toaster oven.

Prep Time and Cooking Time: 12 minutes | Serves:2

Ingredients to Use:

4 mini pitas

½ teaspoon coconut oil

¼ cup ricotta cheese

Pinch ground cinnamon

¼ teaspoon lemon juice

1 tablespoon raspberry preserves

2 peaches, sliced thinly

2 tablespoons blueberries, sliced

Step-by-Step Directions

1.   Preheat your toaster oven to 400 degrees F.
2.   Select toast setting.
3.   Brush both sides of pita with oil.
4.   Add to the toaster oven.
5.   Bake for 4 minutes per side.
6.   In a bowl, mix the ricotta cheese, cinnamon and lemon juice.
7.   Spread ricotta mixture on top of the pita.
8.   Top with the remaining ingredients.
9.   Put the pizzas back to the oven.
10.   Toast for 3 minutes.

Serving Suggestion: Sprinkle with slivered almonds before serving.

Tip: Use whole milk ricotta cheese.

CHAPTER 2: 10 BEEF, PORK, & LAMB RECIPES

Broiled Pork Chops

You can't say no to a dish as delicious and easy to prepare as this one.

Prep Time and Cooking Time: 30 minutes | Serves:2

Ingredients to Use:

2 pork chops

Garlic salt and pepper to taste

Step-by-Step Directions

1. Sprinkle both sides of pork chops with garlic salt and pepper.

2. Place the pork chops inside the toaster oven.

3. Set it to broil.

4. Cook for 15 minutes.

5. Flip and cook for another 10 minutes.

Serving Suggestion: Serve with cabbage and carrot slaw.

Tip: Internal temperature of pork should be at least 145 degrees F.

Beef & Spinach Pie

Prepare this savory pie to turn your day into something extra special.

Prep Time and Cooking Time: 30 minutes | Serves: 8

Ingredients to Use:

¼ cup oats

1 cup all-purpose flour

7 tablespoons butter, sliced into cubes

3 tablespoons cold water

1 onion, chopped

1 clove garlic, minced

1 green bell pepper, chopped

1 lb. ground beef

¼ cup ketchup

½ teaspoon dried basil

1 teaspoon dried oregano

½ teaspoon dried marjoram

Salt and pepper to taste

10 oz. spinach, chopped

3 eggs, beaten

2 cups cheddar cheese, shredded and divided

1 tomato, chopped

Step-by-Step Directions

1. Mix the oats, flour, butter and water in a bowl.

2. Roll into a dough. Transfer to a pie plate.

3. In a pan over medium heat, cook the onion, garlic, bell pepper and beef for 5 minutes. Turn off the heat. Drain fat.

4. Stir in the rest of the ingredients, leaving half of the cheese in a bowl.

5. Top the pie with the beef mixture.

6. Place the pie inside the toaster oven. Set it to bake.

7. Cook at 400 degrees F for 30 minutes.

8. Sprinkle the remaining cheese on top.

9. Bake for another 5 minutes or until cheese has melted.

Serving Suggestion: Let stand for 10 minutes before slicing and serving.

Tip: Use lean ground beef.

Polish Casserole

Combine sausage and pasta in this incredibly easy dish that's ready after a few minutes.

Prep Time and Cooking Time: 45 minutes | Serves: 12

Ingredients to Use:

4 cups penne pasta, cooked according to package directions

1 ½ lb. kielbasa, sliced

4 green onions, chopped

4 cloves garlic, minced

16 oz. sauerkraut, rinsed

1 ¼ cups milk

2 tablespoons Dijon mustard

20 oz. cream of mushroom soup

3 cups Swiss cheese, shredded and divided

Step-by-Step Directions

1. Preheat your oven to 350 degrees F.

2. Set it to bake.

3. Mix all the ingredients in a bowl.

4. Pour the mixture into a baking pan.

5. Bake in the oven for 50 minutes.

Serving Suggestion: Garnish with chopped parsley.

Tip: You can freeze unbaked dish for up to 3 months and thaw overnight in the refrigerator before baking.

Bell Pepper Stuffed with Beef

This can be served as appetizer or as snack.

Prep Time and Cooking Time: 40 minutes | Serves:6

Ingredients to Use:

1 tablespoon olive oil

1 onion, minced

4 cloves garlic, minced

1 lb. lean ground beef

1 zucchini, chopped

2 cups squash, chopped

2 cups fresh spinach, chopped

1 cup brown rice, cooked

8 oz. tomato sauce

Salt to taste

6 large red bell peppers, pre-boiled and tops sliced off

½ cup mozzarella cheese, shredded

Step-by-Step Directions

1.   Pour the oil into a pan over medium heat.

2.   Cook the onion and garlic for 1 minute.

3.   Add the beef.

4.   Cook for 3 to 5 minutes.

5.   Stir in the zucchini and squash.

6.   Cook until tender.

7.   Add the spinach, rice and tomato sauce.

8.   Season with salt.

9.   Turn off the heat.

10.   Stuff the bell peppers with the beef mixture.

11.   Top with the cheese.

12.   Place inside the toaster oven.

13.   Select bake setting.

14.   Cook at 350 degrees F for 20 minutes.

Serving Suggestion: Sprinkle with dried herbs.

Tip: You can also add hot sauce to the mixture.

Burger & Zucchini Pie

You probably wouldn't have guessed that this burger and zucchini pie would taste awesome.

Prep Time and Cooking Time: 1 hour | Serves: 8

Ingredients to Use:

½ lb. ground beef

¼ cup onion, chopped

Salt and pepper to taste

½ cup green pepper, chopped

1 teaspoon dried parsley flakes

1 teaspoon dried oregano

½ cup breadcrumbs

1 egg, beaten

¼ cup Parmesan cheese, grated

4 cups zucchini, sliced

2 tomatoes, sliced thinly

2 refrigerated pie crusts

Step-by-Step Directions

1.   In a pan over medium heat, add the ground beef and onion.

2.   Season with salt and pepper.

3.   Cook for 3 to 5 minutes.

4.   Drain fat.

5.   Stir in the rest of the ingredients except the pie crust.

6.   Place 1 pie crust in a pie pan.

7.   Top with the beef mixture.

8.   Top with the other pie crust

9.   Place inside the toaster oven.

10.   Set it to bake.

11.   Cook at 350 degrees F for 1 hour.

Serving Suggestion: Let cool before slicing and serving.

Tip: Use lean ground beef.

Pepperoni Roll Ups

These pepperoni roll ups are always a big hit. They're easy to make too.

Prep Time and Cooking Time: 20 minutes | Serves:8

Ingredients to Use:

8 oz. refrigerated crescent rolls

16 slices pepperoni, sliced

2 oz. string cheese, sliced

¾ teaspoon Italian seasoning

Garlic salt to taste

Step-by-Step Directions

1.	Separate the dough into 8 triangles.
2.	Top each one with pepperoni and cheese.
3.	Season with herbs and garlic salt.
4.	Roll up the dough.
5.	Add to a baking pan.
6.	Place the baking pan inside the toaster oven.
7.	Choose bake setting.
8.	Bake at 375 degrees F for 10 minutes.

Serving Suggestion: Serve with marinara sauce.

Tip: You can also add chopped bell peppers to the roll ups.

This simple dish will give you your heart's desire.

Prep Time and Cooking Time: 1 hour and 40 minutes | Serves: 6

Ingredients to Use:

1 ½ lb. ground beef

¼ cup onion, chopped

¾ cup oats

¼ cup evaporated milk

1 egg, beaten

½ teaspoon rubbed sage

2 tablespoons Worcestershire sauce

Salt and pepper to taste

¼ cup ketchup

Step-by-Step Directions

1.   Combine all the ingredients except ketchup in a bowl.

2.   Press the mixture into a loaf pan.

3.   Place inside the toaster pan.

4.   Set it to bake.

5.   Cook at 350 degrees F for 1 hour and 15 minutes.

6.   Spread the ketchup on top.

7.   Bake for another 10 minutes.

Serving Suggestion: Let stand for 10 minutes before slicing and serving.

Tip: Use quick cooking oats.

Ham & Vegetable Casserole

You're going to fall in love with this ham and veggie casserole.

Prep Time and Cooking Time: 30 minutes | Serves:4

Ingredients to Use:

2 teaspoons butter

¼ cup breadcrumbs

8 oz. ham, sliced into cubes

16 oz. broccoli florets, steamed

16 oz. cauliflower, steamed

2 tablespoons all-purpose flour

1 ½ cups milk

½ cup Parmesan cheese, grated

Pepper to taste

¾ cup cheddar cheese, shredded

Step-by-Step Directions

1.   Preheat your oven to 425 degrees F.

2.   Set it to bake.

3.   In a pan over medium heat, add the butter and cook breadcrumbs for 2 minutes.

4.   Combine the remaining ingredients in a bowl, topping with the cheddar cheese.

5.   Transfer mixture to a baking pan.

6.   Top with the breadcrumbs.

7.   Bake in the oven for 15 minutes.

Serving Suggestion: Garnish with chopped herbs.

Tip: Use low-fat milk.

Prepare this incredible beef and corn pot pie using your toaster oven.

Prep Time and Cooking Time: 1 hour | Serves: 6

Ingredients to Use:

2 refrigerated pie crust

1 lb. ground beef

1 onion, chopped

¼ cup green bell pepper, chopped

8 oz. tomato sauce

7 oz. corn kernels

1 tablespoon Worcestershire sauce

Salt and pepper to taste

Step-by-Step Directions

1. Roll out 1 pie crust into a pie pan.

2. Set aside the other pie crust.

3. In a pan over medium heat, add the onion, ground beef and bell pepper.

4. Cook for 5 minutes.

5. Stir in the remaining ingredients.

6. Bring to a boil and then simmer for 15 minutes.

7. Add the beef mixture on top of the pie crust.

8. Top with the other pie crust.

9. Place inside the toaster oven.

10. Choose bake function.

11. Cook at 375 degrees F for 15 minutes.

Serving Suggestion: Let cool before slicing and serving.

Tip: Make slits on the top pie crust before baking.

Baked Potato & Beef

The delicious combination of beef and potato make this pie extra memorable.

Prep Time and Cooking Time: 1 hour | Serves: 4

Ingredients to Use:

1 onion, chopped

2 cloves garlic, minced

2 ribs celery, chopped

½ mushrooms, sliced

2 carrots, chopped

1 lb. ground beef

½ lb. pork sausage, crumbled

½ cup orange juice

2 teaspoons orange zest

1 teaspoon ground nutmeg

¼ teaspoon Worcestershire sauce

¼ cup Dijon mustard

2 teaspoons brown sugar

2 teaspoons rice vinegar

Salt and pepper to taste

4 cups mashed potatoes

Step-by-Step Directions

1.   Add the onion, garlic, mushrooms, celery, beef and sausage to a pan over medium heat.

2.   Cook for 10 minutes, stirring often.

3.   Stir in the rest of the ingredients.

4.   Transfer the mixture to a baking pan.

5.   Top with the mashed potatoes.

6.   Slide into the toaster oven.

7.   Set it to bake.

8.   Cook at 350 degrees F for 30 minutes.

Serving Suggestion: Garnish with dried herbs.

Tip: You can also add grated cheddar cheese on top.

CHAPTER 3: 10 FISH & SEAFOOD RECIPES

Miso Salmon

Here's a surprisingly easy salmon recipe that gives you stellar results.

Prep Time and Cooking Time: 4 hours and 10 minutes | Serves: 5

Ingredients to Use:

1 tablespoon soy sauce

¼ cup miso

1/3 cup sake

¼ cup sugar

2 tablespoons vegetable oil

4 salmon fillets

Step-by-Step Directions

1. Combine soy sauce, miso, sake, sugar and oil in a bowl.

2. Coat salmon fillets with the mixture.

3. Cover and refrigerate for 4 hours.

4. Preheat your toaster oven to high.

5. Select broil setting.

6. Place the salmon in the broiler pan.

7. Broil for 5 minutes.

Serving Suggestion: Garnish with sliced cucumbers and tomatoes.

Tip: You can use either red or white miso for this recipe.

Oat & Walnut Salmon

This is a healthy fish that you'd surely love—salmon fillet crusted with oats and walnuts.

Prep Time and Cooking Time: 30 minutes | Serves:2

Ingredients to Use:

2 salmon fillets

Salt and pepper to taste

2 tablespoons olive oil

3 tablespoons walnuts, chopped

3 tablespoons oats

Step-by-Step Directions

1. Preheat your toaster oven to 400 degrees F.

2. Set it to bake.

3. Season salmon with salt and pepper.

4. Mix the remaining ingredients.

5. Press mixture on both sides of salmon.

6. Place the salmon inside the toaster oven.

7. Cook for 15 minutes.

Serving Suggestion: Serve on top of arugula leaves.

Tip: Use skinless salmon for this recipe.

Garlic Parmesan Shrimp

This garlic Parmesan shrimp definitely bursts with flavors you'd love.

Prep Time and Cooking Time: 15 minutes | Serves:4

Ingredients to Use:

Cooking spray

1 lb. shrimp, peeled and deveined

2 tablespoons olive oil

1 tablespoon lemon juice

½ teaspoon dried oregano

½ teaspoon dried basil

4 cloves garlic, minced

¼ cup Parmesan cheese, grated

Salt and pepper to taste

Step-by-Step Directions

1. Preheat your toaster oven to 400 degrees F.

2. Set it to bake.

3. Spray a baking pan with oil.

4. Add the shrimp to the baking pan.

5. In a bowl, combine the remaining ingredients.

6. Pour mixture into the shrimp.

7. Toss to coat evenly.

8. Add the shrimp to the toaster oven.

9. Cook for 7 minutes.

Serving Suggestion: Garnish with chopped parsley.

Tip: Extend cooking time if you'll be using frozen shrimp.

Baked Fish with Asparagus

Bake sole fillet in your toaster oven and serve it with asparagus for a light but satisfying dinner.

Prep Time and Cooking Time: 30 minutes | Serves:2

Ingredients to Use:

Cooking spray

½ lb. asparagus, trimmed

1 tablespoon olive oil

Salt and pepper to taste

2 sole fillets

3 tablespoons Parmesan cheese, grated

1 cup breadcrumbs

Step-by-Step Directions

1. Preheat your toaster oven to 450 degrees F.

2. Select bake setting.

3. Coat asparagus with oil.

4. Season with salt and pepper.

5. Sprinkle both sides of sole with salt and pepper.

6. Dredge with Parmesan cheese and breadcrumbs.

7. Place the fish and asparagus in the toaster oven.

8. Bake for 15 minutes.

Serving Suggestion: Garnish with lemon wedges.

Tip: Do not overcrowd fish in the toaster oven.

Pesto Salmon

Here's a recipe that gives you delicious baked pesto salmon that's ready in less than an hour.

Prep Time and Cooking Time: 30 minutes | Serves:4

Ingredients to Use:

4 salmon fillets

1 tablespoon lemon juice

2 tablespoons pesto

2 tablespoons pine nuts

Step-by-Step Directions

1. Drizzle salmon with lemon juice.

2. Marinate for 15 minutes.

3. Preheat your toaster oven.

4. Choose broiler setting.

5. Set it to high.

6. Spread pesto on top of the salmon.

7. Place it inside the toaster oven.

8. Broil for 15 minutes.

9. Sprinkle with pine nuts and serve.

Serving Suggestion: Serve with cherry tomatoes.

Tip: Extend cooking until there is a brown crust formed.

Broiled Salmon with Zucchini

This is a no-fuss recipe that gives you healthy lunch or dinner.

Prep Time and Cooking Time: 15 minutes | Serves:1

Ingredients to Use:

1 salmon fillet

1 zucchini, sliced into cubes

2 tablespoons olive oil, divided

Salt and pepper to taste

1 tablespoon lemon juice

Step-by-Step Directions

1. Preheat your toaster oven to high.

2. Set it to broil.

3. Drizzle half of oil over the salmon.

4. Toss the zucchini cubes in the remaining oil.

5. Season with salt and pepper.

6. Place the salmon and zucchini inside the toaster oven.

7. Broil for 10 minutes.

8. Drizzle with lemon juice before serving.

Serving Suggestion: Garnish with fresh basil leaves.

Tip: You can also use haddock fillet for this recipe.

Baked Salmon with Corn Salsa

Another refreshing yet easy to prepare dish that you can make with your toaster oven.

Prep Time and Cooking Time: 15 minutes | Serves:2

Ingredients to Use:

Cooking spray

1 bunch asparagus, trimmed

2 salmon fillets

½ cup corn kernels

½ cup tomato, chopped

1 tablespoon olive oil

Salt to taste

2 tablespoons mustard

Step-by-Step Directions

1. Preheat your toaster oven to 450 degrees F.

2. Choose bake function.

3. Spray your baking pan with oil.

4. Place the asparagus on one side of the pan and the salmon in the middle.

5. Mix the tomato and corn kernels in a bowl.

6. Place in the other side of the baking pan.

7. Drizzle salmon and veggies with oil.

8. Season with salt.

9. Spread mustard on top of salmon.

10. Bake in the oven for 15 minutes.

Serving Suggestion: Drizzle with lemon juice before serving.

Tip: Use Dijon style mustard if available.

Mustard Salmon

Top your salmon with creamy sauce for a wonderful lunch or dinner with your family.

Prep Time and Cooking Time: 20 minutes | Serves:4

Ingredients to Use:

4 salmon fillets

Salt and pepper to taste

2 teaspoons Dijon mustard

2 tablespoons breadcrumbs

4 tablespoons creme fraiche

2 tablespoons lemon juice

2 teaspoons chives, chopped

Step-by-Step Directions

1. Line the broiler tray with foil.

2. Place inside the toaster oven.

3. Preheat it to high and set it to broil.

4. Season both sides of salmon with salt and pepper.

5. Spread it with mustard.

6. Dredge with breadcrumbs.

7. Place on top of the broiler tray.

8. Cook for 8 minutes.

9. While waiting, mix the crème fraiche, lemon juice and chives.

10. Serve fish with crème fraiche mixture.

Serving Suggestion: Garnish with chives.

Tip: Sour cream can be used in place of creme fraiche.

Cheesy Fish Fillet

This dish would make you feel like you're in a restaurant!

Prep Time and Cooking Time: 50 minutes | Serves:2

Ingredients to Use:

2 tuna or salmon fillets

1 tablespoon lemon juice

4 cloves garlic, minced

Salt and pepper to taste

¼ cup mayonnaise

1 teaspoon sugar

¼ cup mozzarella cheese, grated

Step-by-Step Directions

1. In a bowl, mix the lemon juice, garlic, salt and pepper.

2. Coat the fish fillets with this mixture.

3. Marinate for 30 minutes.

4. Preheat your toaster oven to 400 degrees F.

5. Choose bake setting.

6. In another bowl, combine mayo and sugar.

7. Place fish on a baking pan.

8. Spread mayo mixture on top.

9. Sprinkle cheese on top of mayo.

10. Slide into the toaster oven.

11. Bake for 10 minutes.

Serving Suggestion: Garnish with chopped parsley or lemon wedges.

Tip: Cook until fish becomes flaky.

Shrimp with Lemon Butter Sauce

Drench shrimp with savory lemon butter sauce for incredible meal you'd enjoy.

Prep Time and Cooking Time: 30 minutes | Serves:4

Ingredients to Use:

1 ¼ lb. shrimp, peeled and deveined

2 tablespoons lemon juice

¼ cup butter, melted

3 cloves garlic, minced

Salt and pepper to taste

Step-by-Step Directions

1. Preheat your toaster oven to 350 degrees.

2. Select bake function.

3. Add the shrimp to a baking pan.

4. Combine remaining ingredients.

5. Pour sauce over the shrimp.

6. Bake the shrimp in the toaster oven for 10 minutes.

Serving Suggestion: Sprinkle with chopped parsley.

Tip: You can also add red pepper flakes to the sauce.

CHAPTER 4: 10 CHICKEN & POULTRY RECIPES

Chicken Club Casserole

Turn your favorite chicken club sandwich into a casserole dish with this simple recipe.

Prep Time and Cooking Time: 40 minutes | Serves: 10

Ingredients to Use:

20 oz. condensed cheddar cheese soup

1 cup mayonnaise

1 cup milk

4 cups chicken, cooked and sliced into cubes

3 cups spinach, chopped

4 tomatoes, chopped

6 cups spiral pasta, cooked according to package directions

1 cup bacon, cooked and crumbled

2 cups Colby-Monterey Jack cheese, shredded

Step-by-Step Directions

1. Preheat your toaster oven to 375 degrees F.

2. Select bake function.

3. In a bowl, mix the cheese soup, mayo, milk, chicken, spinach and tomatoes.

4. Spread pasta in a baking pan.

5. Top with the cheese soup mixture, bacon and cheese.

6. Bake for 40 minutes.

Serving Suggestion:

Tip: You can freeze unbaked casserole for up to 3 months. Thaw in the refrigerator overnight before cooking.

Chicken Cordon Bleu

This is restaurant quality dish that you'd love with every bite.

Prep Time and Cooking Time: 30 minutes | Serves: 2

Ingredients to Use:

2 chicken breast fillets

2 slices ham

2 slices Swiss cheese

½ cup all-purpose flour

Pinch paprika

Salt and pepper to taste

2 tablespoons milk

1 egg

½ cup breadcrumbs

1 tablespoon canola oil

1 tablespoon butter, melted

Step-by-Step Directions

1. Top chicken with ham and Swiss cheese.

2. Roll up and secure with toothpicks.

3. In a bowl, mix flour, paprika, salt and pepper.

4. Coat chicken rolls with this mixture.

5. Dip in a mixture of milk and egg.

6. Dredge with breadcrumbs.

7. In a pan over medium heat, add the oil and cook the chicken until brown on all sides.

8. Place in a baking pan.

9. Put the baking pan inside the toaster oven.

10. Set it to bake.

11. Bake at 350 degrees F for 30 minutes.

12. Drizzle with butter before serving.

Serving Suggestion: Serve with fresh green salad.

Tip: Flatten chicken breast with meat mallet.

Turkey Meatloaf

Once you've tried this amazing recipe, you'll find yourself doing it more often.

Prep Time and Cooking Time: 1 hour | Serves: 8

Ingredients to Use:

Meatloaf

2 lb. ground turkey

1 onion, chopped

½ cup carrot, shredded

1 cup oats

1 egg, beaten

½ cup nonfat milk

2 tablespoons ketchup

1 teaspoon garlic powder

Pepper to taste

Topping

¼ cup ketchup

¼ cup oats

Step-by-Step Directions

1. Preheat your toaster oven to 350 degrees F.

2. Select bake option.

3. Mix the meatloaf ingredients in a bowl.

4. Press mixture into a loaf pan.

5. Bake in the oven for 1 hour.

6. Top with mixture of ketchup and oats.

7. Bake for another 10 minutes.

Serving Suggestion: Let cool before slicing and serving.

Tip: Use quick-cooking oats.

Chicken Reuben Roll Ups

This chicken reuben roll up is not only an eye candy but will also please your taste buds.

Prep Time and Cooking Time: 30 minutes | Serves: 2

Ingredients to Use:

2 chicken breast fillets

¼ teaspoon garlic salt

Pepper to taste

2 slices deli corned beef

2 slices Swiss cheese

2 tablespoons thousand island salad dressing

1 cup breadcrumbs

Step-by-Step Directions

1. Preheat your toaster oven to 425 degrees F.

2. Choose bake setting.

3. Season chicken breast with garlic salt and pepper.

4. Top the chicken breast with corned beef and cheese.

5. Roll up the chicken.

6. Brush with the dressing and dredge with breadcrumbs.

7. Place inside the toaster oven.

8. Bake for 25 minutes.

Serving Suggestion: You can also serve with additional dressing.

Tip: Pound chicken with a meat mallet to flatten.

Chicken Tater Bake

This dish is simple to prepare yet will surely please everyone at the dinner table.

Prep Time and Cooking Time: 50 minutes | Serves: 12

Ingredients to Use:

½ cup milk

20 oz. condensed cream of chicken soup

¼ cup butter, sliced into cubes

3 cups chicken, shredded and sliced into cubes

1 ½ cups cheddar cheese, shredded and divided

16 oz. frozen peas and carrots

32 oz. frozen tater tots

Step-by-Step Directions

1. Add the milk, soup and butter to a pan over medium heat.

2. Cook while stirring for 10 minutes.

3. Turn off heat.

4. Stir in the chicken, half of cheese and frozen veggies.

5. Transfer to a baking pan.

6. Top with the frozen tater tots.

7. Place inside the toaster oven.

8. Set it to 400 degrees F.

9. Bake for 30 minutes.

10. Top with remaining cheese.

11. Bake for another 10 minutes.

Serving Suggestion: Garnish with chopped green onions.

Tip: Uncooked casserole can be frozen for up to 3 months.

Turkey Pot Pie

Here's a recipe that you'd want to try the next time your friends are coming over.

Prep Time and Cooking Time: 40 minutes | Serves: 6

Ingredients to Use:

2 refrigerated pie crust

½ cup onion, chopped

½ cup celery, chopped

1 cup carrots, sliced into cubes

2 cups potatoes, sliced into cubes

1 ½ cups chicken broth

1 ½ cups milk

¼ cup all-purpose flour

4 cups turkey breast, cooked and sliced into cubes

2 cups cheddar cheese, shredded

¼ teaspoon poultry seasoning

Salt and pepper to taste

Step-by-Step Directions

1. Simmer onion, celery, carrots and potatoes in chicken broth for 10 minutes.

2. Mix milk and flour in a bowl.

3. Pour mixture into the pot with vegetables.

4. Cook while stirring for 3 minutes.

5. Add the turkey, cheese, poultry seasoning, salt and pepper.

6. Cook until the cheese has melted.

7. Place the pie crust in a pie pan.

8. Top with the turkey mixture. Top with the other pie crust.

9. Seal the edges. Place inside the toaster oven.

10. Choose bake function.

11. Bake in the toaster oven at 425 degrees F for 40 minutes.

Serving Suggestion: Let cool before slicing and serving.

Tip: Use sharp cheddar cheese.

Turkey Tetrazzini with Mushrooms

No one will suspect that this is a super simple dish that only takes a few minutes to prepare.

Prep Time and Cooking Time: 40 minutes | Serves: 6

Ingredients to Use:

1 tablespoon butter

¼ cup onion, chopped

1 clove garlic, minced

15 oz. chicken broth

3 tablespoons cornstarch

Salt and pepper to taste

12 oz. evaporated milk

2 ½ cups turkey breast, cooked

6 cups spaghetti, cooked

4 oz. mushrooms

¼ teaspoon paprika

2 tablespoons Parmesan cheese, grated

Step-by-Step Directions

1. Add butter to a pan over medium heat.

2. Cook onion and garlic for 1 minute.

3. Mix broth, cornstarch, salt and pepper in a bowl.

4. Pour mixture into the pan. Bring to a boil.

5. Reduce heat and simmer for 2 minutes.

6. Stir in the milk, turkey, pasta and mushrooms.

7. Turn off heat. Transfer mixture to a baking pan.

8. Place the baking pan inside the toaster oven.

9. Choose bake setting.

10. Cook at 350 degrees F for 20 minutes.

11. Take the pan out of the oven.

12. Sprinkle with paprika and cheese.

13. Bake for another 10 minutes.

Serving Suggestion: Sprinkle with dried herbs.

Tip: Use low-sodium chicken broth.

Turkey Casserole

You'll love how easy and flavorful this turkey casserole is.

Prep Time and Cooking Time: 1 hour | Serves: 6

Ingredients to Use:

1 onion, chopped

2 ribs celery, chopped

2 cups potatoes, diced

2 teaspoons chicken bouillon granules

½ teaspoon dried rosemary, crushed

¼ teaspoon garlic powder

¼ teaspoon dried thyme

½ cup water

15 oz. chicken broth

Pepper to taste

2/3 cup evaporated milk

3 tablespoons all-purpose flour

2 cups turkey breast, cooked and shredded

3 cups frozen mixed vegetables

1 refrigerated pie crust, torn

Step-by-Step Directions

1. Preheat your oven to 400 degrees F. Select bake setting.

2. Combine onion, celery, potatoes, chicken bouillon granules, herbs, spices, water, broth and pepper in a pan over medium heat.

3. Bring to a boil. Reduce heat.

4. Simmer for 15 minutes.

5. Stir in milk and flour.

6. Cook for 2 minutes.

7. Add turkey and veggies.

8. Cook for another 3 minutes.

9. Transfer mixture to a baking pan.

10. Top with pie crust.

11. Place baking pan inside the toaster oven.

12. Cook for 20 minutes.

Serving Suggestion: Let sit for 10 minutes before serving.

Tip: Use non-fat evaporated milk

Chicken Casserole Salsa Verde

This Tex-Mex dish will surely make everyone at the dinner table go wow.

Prep Time and Cooking Time: 30 minutes | Serves: 6

Ingredients to Use:

2 cups rotisserie chicken, cooked and shredded

2 cups salsa verde, divided

1 cup sour cream

8 corn tortillas

2 cups tomatoes, chopped

2 cups Monterey Jack cheese, shredded

Step-by-Step Directions

1. Mix chicken, half of salsa and sour cream in a baking pan.

2. Top with the tortillas.

3. Top with another layer of tomatoes and cheese.

4. Place inside the toaster oven.

5. Choose bake setting.

6. Bake at 400 degrees F for 20 minutes.

7. Serve with remaining salsa.

Serving Suggestion: Serve with fresh cilantro and avocado slices.

Tip: You can also use flour tortillas.

Baked Garlic Chicken

You don't have to make a big fuss when friends are coming over when you have a reliable recipe like this one.

Prep Time and Cooking Time: 40 minutes | Serves: 2

Ingredients to Use:

2 chicken breast fillets

2 tablespoons olive oil

6 cloves garlic, minced

Salt and pepper to taste

Step-by-Step Directions

1. Brush both sides of chicken breast fillets with oil.

2. Sprinkle with garlic, salt and pepper.

3. Place inside the toaster oven.

4. Select bake function.

5. Cook at 400 degrees F for 30 minutes.

Serving Suggestion: Garnish with chopped parsley.

Tip: You can also use turkey breast fillet for this recipe.

CHAPTER 5: 10 VEGAN & VEGETARIAN RECIPES

Baked Veggie Casserole

This is as delicious and appetizing as you imagine it to be.

Prep Time and Cooking Time: 45 minutes | Serves: 6

Ingredients to Use:

2 lb. Brussels sprouts, sliced into wedges

1 tablespoon olive oil

Salt and pepper to taste

1 tablespoon butter

¾ cup sourdough bread, sliced into cubes

2 cloves garlic, minced

1 tablespoon fresh parsley, chopped

1 cup heavy whipping cream

Pinch red pepper flakes

Pinch ground nutmeg

½ cup Swiss cheese, shredded

Step-by-Step Directions

1. Preheat your toaster oven to 450 degrees F. Choose bake setting.

2. Toss Brussels sprouts in oil, salt and pepper.

3. Put these in a baking pan. Place inside the toaster oven.

4. Bake for 10 minutes. Reduce temperature to 400 degrees F.

5. Add butter, bread, garlic and parsley to a food processor.

6. Pulse until crumbly.

7. Add this to the Brussels sprouts along with the rest of the ingredients.

8. Bake for 20 minutes.

Serving Suggestion: Serve immediately.

Tip: You can also use provolone cheese.

Asparagus

Cook asparagus spears inside your toaster oven for a simple and light side dish.

Prep Time and Cooking Time: 1 hour and 20 minutes | Serves:4

Ingredients to Use:

1 bunch asparagus

5 tablespoons olive oil

Salt and pepper to taste

Step-by-Step Directions

1. Spread asparagus in a baking pan.

2. Drizzle with olive oil.

3. Season with salt and pepper.

4. Preheat your toaster oven to high.

5. Set it to broil.

6. Cook for 5 to 10 minutes.

Serving Suggestion: Serve with favorite dipping sauce.

Tip: Don't overcook as you want the asparagus to be crunchy.

Lentil Loaf

This lentil loaf is packed with nutrients and delicious flavors.

Prep Time and Cooking Time: 2 hours | Serves: 6

Ingredients to Use:

14 oz. vegetable broth

¾ cup brown lentils, rinsed

1 tablespoon olive oil

2 cups carrots, shredded

1 onion, chopped

1 cup mushrooms, chopped

2 teaspoons dried basil

1 tablespoon fresh parsley, minced

1 cup mozzarella cheese, shredded

½ cup brown rice, cooked

2 eggs, beaten

Salt and pepper to taste

½ teaspoon garlic powder

2 tablespoons tomato paste

2 tablespoons water

Step-by-Step Directions

1. Pour broth into a pot over medium heat.

2. Add lentils and cook for 30 minutes.

3. Drain and set aside.

4. In a pan over medium heat, cook onion, mushrooms and carrots for 10 minutes.

5. Stir in the herbs.

6. Transfer to a bowl.

7. Stir in the lentils and the rest of the ingredients.

8. Mix well.

9. Transfer mixture into a loaf pan.

10. Place inside the toaster oven.

11. Set it to bake.

12. Cook at 320 degrees F for 1 hour.

Serving Suggestion: Let stand for 10 minutes before slicing.

Tip: Use low-sodium vegetable broth.

Sugar Snap Peas

Simple but delightful—these sugar snap peas will not disappoint.

Prep Time and Cooking Time: 30 minutes | Serves: 2

Ingredients to Use:

8 oz. sugar snap peas

1 tablespoon shallot, chopped

2 teaspoons olive oil

½ teaspoon Italian seasoning

Salt to taste

Step-by-Step Directions

1. Preheat your oven to 400 degrees F.

2. Select bake function.

3. Combine all the ingredients in a baking pan.

4. Place inside the toaster oven.

5. Cook for 10 minutes, stirring once.

Serving Suggestion: Sprinkle with Parmesan cheese.

Tip: You can also add minced garlic to the mixture.

Scalloped Potatoes

This will excite you to no end—rich and creamy potatoes baked in the toaster oven.

Prep Time and Cooking Time: 1 hour and 15 minutes | Serves: 6

Ingredients to Use:

2 tablespoons butter

1 ½ cups milk

Salt and pepper to taste

3 tablespoons all-purpose flour

½ cup cheddar cheese, shredded

2 lb. potatoes, sliced thinly

1 cup onions, sliced thinly

Step-by-Step Directions

1. Preheat your oven to 350 degrees F.
2. Choose bake setting.
3. Add the butter to a pan over medium heat.
4. Stir in milk, salt, pepper and flour.
5. Bring to a boil.
6. Turn off heat.
7. Add the cheese.
8. Spread potatoes in the baking pan.
9. Top with the onions and milk mixture.
10. Bake in the oven for 50 minutes while covered.
11. Uncover and bake for another 10 minutes.

Serving Suggestion: Garnish with chopped parsley.

Tip: Use low-fat milk and cheese.

Cauliflower with Brown Butter Sauce

Cauliflower has never tasted this good!

Prep Time and Cooking Time: 30 minutes | Serves: 4

Ingredients to Use:

3 tablespoons butter

6 cloves garlic, minced

4 cups cauliflower florets

Salt and pepper to taste

Step-by-Step Directions

1. Preheat your oven to 400 degrees F.

2. Select bake function.

3. Add butter to a pan over medium heat.

4. Cook garlic for 1 minute or until butter has browned a little.

5. Turn off heat.

6. Toss cauliflower in brown butter and garlic.

7. Transfer to baking pan.

8. Season with salt and pepper.

9. Bake in the oven for 20 minutes.

Serving Suggestion: Garnish with chopped herbs.

Tip: Add capers to the mixture.

Squash Mac & Cheese

Enjoy this creamy mac and cheese recipe with butternut squash.

Prep Time and Cooking Time: 40 minutes | Serves: 6

Ingredients to Use:

1 butternut squash, sliced into cubes and boiled

6 cups elbow macaroni, cooked according to package directions

¼ cup yogurt

1 cup milk

Salt and pepper to taste

Pinch ground nutmeg

6 oz. cheddar cheese, shredded

½ cup Parmesan cheese, shredded

½ cup breadcrumbs

Step-by-Step Directions

1. Preheat your toaster oven to 400 degrees F.

2. Choose bake setting.

3. Puree the squash in a food processor.

4. Combine all the ingredients in a baking pan along with the pureed squash.

5. Bake for 20 minutes.

Serving Suggestion: Sprinkle with chopped herbs.

Tip: Use plain Greek yogurt.

Spaghetti Casserole

This is another way to cook your favorite spaghetti. For sure, you'll love this just as much.

Prep Time and Cooking Time: 30 minutes | Serves: 4

Ingredients to Use:

½ cup onion, chopped

1 teaspoon garlic, minced

1 cup green bell pepper, chopped

Salt and pepper to taste

45 oz. spaghetti in tomato sauce

6 oz. mushrooms

2 oz. olives, sliced

2 cups cheddar cheese, shredded

1 cup Parmesan cheese, grated

Step-by-Step Directions

1. Add the onion, garlic, bell pepper, salt and pepper to a pan over medium heat.

2. Cook for 10 minutes, stirring often.

3. Transfer mixture to a baking pan.

4. Stir in the rest of the ingredients except the cheeses.

5. Top with the cheeses.

6. Slide into the toaster oven.

7. Bake at 350 degrees F for 30 minutes.

Serving Suggestion: Garnish with chopped basil.

Tip: You can also use veggie meat if you like.

Smoky Cauliflower

You'll love the smoky flavor from this baked cauliflower dish.

Prep Time and Cooking Time: 30 minutes | Serves: 4

Ingredients to Use:

3 tablespoons olive oil

4 cups cauliflower florets

1 teaspoon paprika

¼ teaspoon ground turmeric

½ teaspoon ground cumin

Pinch chili powder

Salt and pepper to taste

Step-by-Step Directions

1. Preheat your toaster oven to 450 degrees F.

2. Select bake setting.

3. Combine all the ingredients in a baking pan.

4. Place inside the toaster oven.

5. Cook for 20 minutes.

Serving Suggestion: Serve with spicy mayo dip.

Tip: You can also use broccoli for this recipe.

Spicy Green Beans

This is another great idea for side dish that you can prepare when running out of time.

Prep Time and Cooking Time: 30 minutes | Serves: 4

Ingredients to Use:

4 cups green beans, trimmed and sliced

1 teaspoon olive oil

1 tablespoon lemon juice

Pinch chili powder

Step-by-Step Directions

1. Toss green beans in oil and lemon juice.

2. Sprinkle with chili powder.

3. Spread in the baking pan.

4. Place inside the toaster oven.

5. Bake at 400 degrees F for 5 to 10 minutes, stirring once.

Serving Suggestion: Sprinkle with crispy garlic flakes.

Tip: You can also use hot pepper sauce instead of chili powder.

CHAPTER 6: 10 SOUPS, STEWS & BROTH RECIPES

Baked Vegetable Soup

This peasant-style Italian soup is sure to please your heart and tummy.

Prep Time and Cooking Time: 1 hour and 40 minutes | Serves:8

Ingredients to Use:

5 tablespoons olive oil

1 lb. potato, sliced into cubes

Salt to taste

2 stalks celery, sliced thinly

10 oz. mushrooms, sliced

2 leeks, sliced

2 zucchini, sliced

¼ cup fresh parsley, chopped

15 oz. canned tomatoes

6 cups water

2 tablespoons Parmesan cheese, grated

Pepper to taste

Step-by-Step Directions

1. Preheat your oven to 350 degrees F.

2. Add oil to a small pot over medium heat.

3. Layer the potatoes at the bottom of the pot.

4. Top with the celery, mushrooms, leeks and zucchini.

5. Season with salt.

6. Sprinkle with parsley.

7. Spread the tomatoes on top.

8. Pour in the water.

9. Sprinkle with Parmesan cheese and pepper.

10. Bring to a boil.

11. Transfer to the toaster oven.

12. Set it to bake.

13. Cook for 1 hour.

Serving Suggestion: Sprinkle with chopped parsley.

Tip: Swish sliced leeks in a bowl of water to get rid of soil or sand trapped in the layers.

Baked Potato Soup

You'll love this creamy and delicious baked potato soup.

Prep Time and Cooking Time: 45 minutes | Serves: 8

Ingredients to Use:

4 cups water

2 lb. potatoes, sliced into wedges

¾ teaspoon salt

2 tablespoons butter

1 yellow onion

3 cloves garlic, minced

¼ cup flour

3 cups chicken broth

2 cups half and half

¾ cup sour cream

Pepper to taste

2 cups cheddar cheese, shredded

6 slices bacon, cooked crisp and crumbled

Step-by-Step Directions

1. Pour water into a pot over medium heat.

2. Add the potatoes and salt.

3. Boil until tender.

4. Drain the potatoes and mash with a fork. Set aside.

5. In a pan over medium heat, add the butter and let it melt.

6. Cook onion and garlic for 1 minute.

7. Stir in flour, broth, half and half, mashed potatoes, sour cream and pepper.

8. Add the cheese and stir.

9. Transfer to the toaster oven.

10. Select bake setting.

11. Bake at 350 degrees F for 5 minutes.

12. Sprinkle with bacon and serve.

Serving Suggestion: Garnish with chopped chives.

Tip: Use large Russet potatoes.

Beef & Vegetable Stew

This is comfort food in a bowl!

Prep Time and Cooking Time: 2 hours | Serves: 8

Ingredients to Use:

1 tablespoon olive oil

1 ½ lb. beef, sliced

3 ribs celery, chopped

1 onion, chopped

4 cups water

28 oz. beef broth

14 oz. canned whole tomatoes

14 oz. canned crushed tomatoes

2 potatoes, sliced into cubes

2 carrots, sliced into cubes

2 teaspoons garlic powder

2 bay leaves

1 cup corn kernels

1 cup green beans

2 teaspoons hot pepper sauce

Step-by-Step Directions

1. Pour oil into a small pot over medium heat.

2. Cook beef for 5 minutes.

3. Transfer beef to a plate.

4. Cook onion and celery in beef dripping for 5 minutes.

5. Put beef back to the pot along with the rest of the ingredients.

6. Bring to a boil.

7. Transfer the pot to the toaster oven.

8. Cook at 350 degrees F for 1 hour.

Serving Suggestion: Sprinkle with pepper.

Tip: Use beef top sirloin if available.

Baked Stew

Stew baked in the toaster oven? Yes, it's possible, and delicious too.

Prep Time and Cooking Time: 2 hours and 15 minutes | Serves: 6

Ingredients to Use:

2 lb. stew meat, cubed

¼ cup all-purpose flour

2 tablespoons vegetable oil

14 oz. canned tomatoes

5 carrots, sliced into cubes

3 potatoes, sliced into cubes

10 oz. frozen peas

1 ½ cups water

1 packet dry onion soup mix

Salt and pepper to taste

Step-by-Step Directions

1. Preheat your oven to 400 degrees F.

2. Select bake setting.

3. Coat the beef in flour.

4. Pour oil into a roasting pan.

5. Spread the meat in the pan.

6. Bake the beef for 30 minutes.

7. Stir in the rest of the ingredients.

8. Reduce temperature to 375 degrees F.

9. Cook for 2 hours.

Serving Suggestion: Sprinkle with pepper and dried herbs.

Tip: You can also add sliced sausages to the soup.

Baked Veggie Soup

You'll love the flavor of this soup that has just the right balance of sweet and savory.

Prep Time and Cooking Time: 1 hour and 15 minutes | Serves: 8

Ingredients to Use:

1 eggplant, sliced in half

4 cups cauliflower florets

2 onions, sliced into wedges

2 red bell peppers, sliced in half

4 cloves garlic

3 tomatoes, sliced into wedges

1 zucchini, sliced

5 carrots, chopped

2 tablespoons olive oil

Salt and pepper to taste

5 cups vegetable stock

1 cup coconut milk

Step-by-Step Directions

1. Preheat your oven to 400 degrees F.

2. Select bake setting.

3. Spread the vegetables in the baking pan.

4. Drizzle with the olive oil.

5. Season with salt and pepper.

6. Slide into the toaster oven.

7. Cook for 40 minutes.

8. Add veggies to a food processor.

9. Transfer to a pot.

10. Stir in remaining ingredients.

11. Simmer in the pot for 20 minutes.

Serving Suggestion: Top with yogurt.

Tip: Freeze in container for up to 1 to 2 months.

French Beef Stew

This is the kind of soup that will surely warm you up on a chilly night.

Prep Time and Cooking Time: 3 hours and 30 minutes | Serves: 6

Ingredients to Use:

3 lb. beef chuck, sliced into cubes

Salt and pepper to taste

3 tablespoons olive oil

2 yellow onion, sliced into chunks

7 cloves garlic, crushed

2 tablespoons balsamic vinegar

1 ½ tablespoons tomato paste

½ teaspoon dried thyme

1 ½ teaspoons sugar

4 carrots, sliced into cubes

1 lb. potatoes

¼ cup all purpose flour

2 cups red wine

2 cups beef broth

2 cups water

1 bay leaf

Step-by-Step Directions

1. Preheat your oven to 325 degrees F.

2. Season with salt and pepper.

3. In a pot over medium heat, add olive oil.

4. Cook beef until browned on all sides.

5. Stir in onion and garlic.

6. Pour in balsamic vinegar.

7. Cook for 5 minutes.

8. Stir in the rest of the ingredients.

9. Bring to a boil. Cover the pot.

10. Place inside the toaster oven.

11. Cook for 3 hours.

Serving Suggestion: Discard bay leaf before serving.

Tip: Flavor is more intense when you make it 1 day ahead and refrigerate until next day.

Cheesy Potato Stew

With a recipe like this, you can't go wrong with your lunch or dinner.

Prep Time and Cooking Time: 1 hour and 30 minutes | Serves: 4

Ingredients to Use:

3 tablespoons butter

2 cups onion, chopped

1 tablespoons garlic, minced

1 cup celery, chopped

1 cup carrot, chopped

¼ teaspoon dried rosemary

¼ cup red pepper flakes

Salt and pepper to taste

4 cups chicken broth

3 tablespoons flour

3 potatoes, sliced into cubes

1 bay leaf

¼ cup sour cream

1 cup cheddar cheese, shredded

Step-by-Step Directions

1. Add the butter to a pot over medium heat.

2. Cook onion, garlic, celery and carrots for 5 minutes, stirring often.

3. Season with rosemary, red pepper flakes, salt and pepper.

4. Cook for 30 seconds.

5. Add broth and flour.

6. Cook while for 1 minute.

7. Stir in the remaining ingredients.

8. Bring to a boil.

9. Transfer to the toaster oven.

10. Select bake setting.

11. Cook at 350 degrees F for 1 hour.

Serving Suggestion: Garnish with chopped chives.

Tip: Use low-sodium chicken broth.

Pumpkin Soup

This is a simple, no-fail pumpkin soup recipe that you'd enjoy preparing for your family.

Prep Time and Cooking Time: 1 hour and 10 minutes | Serves:6

Ingredients to Use:

2 pumpkins, sliced into cubes

1 tablespoon olive oil

12 oz. dry white wine

¾ cup butter

3 ½ cups water

1 teaspoon garlic powder

Salt and pepper to taste

Step-by-Step Directions

1. Preheat your toaster oven to 450°F.

2. Add pumpkin cubes to a baking sheet.

3. Drizzle with oil.

4. Add to the toaster oven.

5. Select bake function.

6. Cook for 45 minutes.

7. Transfer to the food processor.

8. Pulse until smooth.

9. Transfer to a soup pot.

10. Stir in the rest of the ingredients.

11. Simmer for 10 minutes.

Serving Suggestion: Garnish with pumpkin seeds.

Tip: You can also brown the pumpkin seeds in butter before using as garnish.

Baked Bean Soup

Prepare this bean soup ahead of time and reheat whenever you're having a busy day.

Prep Time and Cooking Time: 4 hours and 50 minutes | Serves: 14

Ingredients to Use:

1 lb. dried navy beans

1 ¼ lb. ham, cooked and diced

3 qt. water

16 oz. tomato sauce

1 cup onion, diced

1 cup celery, diced

1 cup carrot, diced

2 teaspoons chili powder

1 teaspoon dried marjoram

Salt and pepper to taste

Step-by-Step Directions

1. Put all the ingredients in a baking pan.

2. Cover the baking pan with foil.

3. Place inside the toaster oven.

4. Select bake setting.

5. Cook at 350 degrees F for 4 hours and 30 minutes.

Serving Suggestion: Sprinkle with chopped fresh basil.

Tip: Soak dry navy beans in a bowl of water for a few hours.

Carrot Soup

Cook the carrot in toaster oven before turning it in soup.

Prep Time and Cooking Time: 1 hour and 20 minutes | Serves: 6

Ingredients to Use:

6 carrots, sliced

1 yellow onion, sliced thinly

4 cloves garlic, peeled

2 tablespoons olive oil

1 teaspoon ground cumin

Salt and pepper to taste

56 oz. canned tomatoes

1 teaspoon dried basil

½ cup plain Greek yogurt

Step-by-Step Directions

1. Preheat your toaster oven to 400 degrees F.
2. Choose bake function.
3. In a bowl, add the onion, garlic and carrots.
4. Drizzle with oil.
5. Season with cumin, salt and pepper.
6. Spread in a baking pan.
7. Bake for 30 minutes.
8. Let cool.
9. Transfer to a food processor.
10. Pulse until pureed.
11. Transfer to a pot over medium heat.
12. Stir in the rest of the ingredients.
13. Simmer for 30 minutes.

Serving Suggestion: Garnish with fresh basil.

Tip: Refrigerate for up to 5 days.

CHAPTER 7: 10 BEANS AND EGGS RECIPES

Baked Eggs with Marinara & Parmesan Cheese

These tasty eggs can be served for breakfast, snack or whenever you're craving for something healthy and flavorful.

Prep Time and Cooking Time: 30 minutes | Serves: 4

Ingredients to Use:

Butter

8 eggs

1 cup marinara sauce

¼ cup whipping cream

¼ cup Parmesan cheese, grated

Salt and pepper to taste

Step-by-Step Directions

1. Brush 4 ramekins with butter.

2. Spread marinara at the bottom of the ramekins.

3. Crack an egg into each of the ramekins.

4. Top the eggs with the cream and cheese.

5. Season with salt and pepper.

6. Place inside the toaster oven.

7. Set it to bake.

8. Cook at 400 degrees F for 15 minutes.

Serving Suggestion: Garnish with chopped chives.

Tip: Use low-sodium marinara sauce.

This is the kind of baked egg dish that will make you feel like your taste buds are in heaven.

Prep Time and Cooking Time: 15 minutes | Serves: 2

Ingredients to Use:

2 eggs

2 teaspoons butter

2 slices bread

Pepper to taste

Step-by-Step Directions

1. Preheat your toaster oven to high.

2. Set it to broil.

3. Crack the eggs into 2 ramekins.

4. Cook the eggs until the whites are firm.

5. Spread bread with butter.

6. Top with the cooked eggs.

7. Sprinkle with pepper.

8. Choose toast setting.

9. Toast the bread with egg for 5 minutes.

Serving Suggestion: Sprinkle with dried herbs.

Tip: Use whole-wheat bread.

Baked Eggs with Fontina Cheese

Creamy and cheesy, this is a delicious snack you'd love to eat more often.

Prep Time and Cooking Time: 30 minutes | Serves: 2

Ingredients to Use:

Olive oil

4 eggs

½ cup tomato sauce

2 tablespoons heavy cream

2 tablespoons fontina cheese, grated

Salt and pepper to taste

Step-by-Step Directions

1. Preheat your toaster oven to 425 degrees F.
2. Select bake setting.
3. Grease ramekins with oil.
4. Pour tomato sauce into the ramekins.
5. Crack 2 eggs into each ramekin.
6. Top with cream and cheese.
7. Season with salt and pepper.
8. Place the ramekins inside the toaster oven.
9. Cook for 20 minutes.

Serving Suggestion: Garnish with fresh herbs.

Tip: Use low-sodium tomato sauce.

Cheesy Eggs Toast

You'll love the creamy eggs and crunchy grated cheese on toasted bread.

Prep Time and Cooking Time: 30 minutes | Serves: 2

Ingredients to Use:

2 slices bread

1 tablespoon butter

2 eggs

Salt and pepper to taste

1 cup cheddar cheese, shredded

Cooking spray

Step-by-Step Directions

1. Press down the center of the bread.

2. Spread with butter.

3. Crack the eggs on top of the bread.

4. Sprinkle the cheese around the eggs.

5. Season with salt and pepper.

6. Spray with oil.

7. Place inside the toaster oven.

8. Set it to toast.

9. Toast at 350 degrees F for 10 minutes.

Serving Suggestion: Sprinkle with dried herbs.

Tip: Cook until edges have browned.

Black Bean Tostada

This snack is not only filling but also full of flavor.

Prep Time and Cooking Time: 30 minutes | Serves: 2

Ingredients to Use:

2 corn tortillas

1 clove garlic, minced

1 cup black beans, cooked

½ teaspoon ground cumin

¼ teaspoon smoked paprika

Salt and pepper to taste

1 tomato, chopped

¼ cup cheddar cheese, shredded

Step-by-Step Directions

1. Add the corn tortillas to the toaster oven.

2. Choose toast setting.

3. Toast at 375 degrees F for 2 minutes.

4. In a bowl, mash the beans and mix with the spices, salt and pepper.

5. Top the tortillas with the bean mixture.

6. Sprinkle with tomato and cheese.

7. Put these back to the oven.

8. Toast for 10 minutes.

Serving Suggestion: Top with avocado slices and chopped jalapeño.

Tip: Use Romaine lettuce if available.

Baked Beans

Healthy and delicious, these baked beans are always a delight.

Prep Time and Cooking Time: 1 hour | Serves: 6

Ingredients to Use:

30 oz. canned baked beans with pork

½ cup brown sugar

½ cup ketchup

1 tablespoon Worcestershire sauce

Step-by-Step Directions

1. Preheat your toaster oven to 350 degrees F.

2. Select bake function.

3. Combine all the ingredients in a baking pan.

4. Bake in the oven for 45 minutes.

Serving Suggestion: Serve warm.

Tip: You can also season with pepper.

Bean & Cheese Burrito

Here's a healthy snack everyone at home will love.

Prep Time and Cooking Time: 15 minutes | Serves: 2

Ingredients to Use:

2 corn tortillas

½ cup black beans or pinto beans, cooked

1 oz. mozzarella cheese

1 cup salsa

Step-by-Step Directions

1. Preheat your toaster oven to 350 degrees F.

2. Choose toast setting.

3. Top the tortillas with the beans, cheese and salsa.

4. Roll up and place inside the toaster oven.

5. Toast for 5 minutes.

Serving Suggestion: Serve with hot sauce and sour cream.

Tip: You can also use flour tortillas for this recipe.

Toasted Chickpeas

Toast your seasoned chickpeas in the toaster oven for a quick and healthy snack.

Prep Time and Cooking Time: 30 minutes | Serves: 6

Ingredients to Use:

3 cups chickpeas, rinsed and drained

1 tablespoon olive oil

¼ teaspoon cumin

Salt to taste

Step-by-Step Directions

1. Preheat your oven to 400 degrees F.

2. Select bake setting.

3. Drizzle chickpeas with oil.

4. Season with cumin and salt.

5. Bake in the toaster oven for 15 minutes.

6. Reduce oven temperature to 350 degrees F.

7. Cook for 10 minutes.

Serving Suggestion: Let cool before serving or storing.

Tip: Store in an airtight container for up to 1 week.

Bean & Cheese Quesadilla

This is actually easier to prepare than it looks.

Prep Time and Cooking Time: 20 minutes | Serves: 1

Ingredients to Use:

2 flour tortillas

¼ cup refried beans

1 tablespoon jalapeño, chopped

¼ cup Mexican cheese blend, shredded

Step-by-Step Directions

1. Spread the refried beans, jalapeño and cheese on top of the tortilla.

2. Top with the other tortilla.

3. Place the quesadillas inside the toaster oven.

4. Set it to toast.

5. Cook at 350 degrees F for 5 minutes.

6. Let cool before slicing and serving.

Serving Suggestion: Serve with salsa.

Tip: You can also make your own flour tortilla with flour, salt, water and olive oil.

Cheesy Scrambled Eggs

Combine egg and cheese in this toaster oven dish that only takes a few minutes to prepare.

Prep Time and Cooking Time: 35 minutes | Serves: 12

Ingredients to Use:

24 eggs, beaten

½ cup butter, melted

2 ½ cups milk

2 ¼ teaspoons salt

Step-by-Step Directions

1. Preheat your toaster oven to 350 degrees F.

2. Select bake option.

3. Combine all the ingredients in a baking pan.

4. Cook in the toaster oven for 10 minutes.

5. Stir and cook for another 15 minutes.

Serving Suggestion: Garnish with chopped green onion.

Tip: You can also use almond milk if you prefer non-dairy.

CHAPTER 8: 10 DESSERTS AND SNACK RECIPES

Cinnamon Oatmeal Cookies

A no-guilt dessert recipe that you can enjoy anytime.

Prep Time and Cooking Time: 1 hour | Serves: 24

Ingredients to Use:

Cooking spray

1 ½ cups all-purpose flour

2 cups old fashioned oats

½ teaspoon baking soda

½ teaspoon baking powder

1 tablespoon cinnamon

½ cup butter

1 teaspoon vanilla

¼ cup white sugar

½ cup brown sugar

1 egg, beaten

½ teaspoon salt

Step-by-Step Directions

1. Preheat your toaster oven to 350 degrees F.

2. Choose bake setting.

3. Spray your baking pan with oil.

4. Combine all the ingredients in a bowl.

5. Form cookies from the mixture.

6. Place in the baking pan.

7. Add to the toaster oven.

8. Bake for 15 minutes.

Serving Suggestion: Serve with milk.

Tip: Let cool on a wire rack for 15 minutes before serving.

Bread Pudding

This dessert recipe is super simple and will only require minimal effort.

Prep Time and Cooking Time: 1 hour | Serves: 12

Ingredients to Use:

2 cups evaporated milk

1 cup condensed milk

1 loaf bread, sliced

Step-by-Step Directions

1. Preheat your toaster oven to 400 degrees F.

2. Select bake setting.

3. Grease your baking pan.

4. Mix evaporated and condensed milk.

5. Soak the bread in milk mixture.

6. Place the bread in the baking pan.

7. Cook for 15 minutes.

Serving Suggestion: Sprinkle with grated cheese.

Tip: You can use sugar instead of condensed milk.

Chocolate Cookies

Enjoy every bite of these creamy and decadent chocolate cookies.

Prep Time and Cooking Time: 30 minutes | Serves: 6

Ingredients to Use:

1 ½ tablespoons butter

3 tablespoons brown sugar

1 egg yolk

¼ teaspoon vanilla extract

¼ cup all-purpose flour

¼ teaspoon baking soda

2 tablespoons cocoa

3 tablespoons chocolate chips

Pinch salt

Step-by-Step Directions

1. Beat sugar and butter using a mixer for 2 minutes.

2. Stir in vanilla and egg yolk.

3. Transfer mixture to a bowl.

4. Stir in the rest of the ingredients.

5. Refrigerate dough for 10 minutes.

6. Form cookies from the mixture and place on a baking pan.

7. Set your toaster oven to bake.

8. Set the temperature to 350 degrees F.

9. Bake the cookies in the toaster oven for 5 to 10 minutes.

Serving Suggestion: Let cool before serving.

Tip: Store in an airtight container at room temperature for up to 3 days.

Fruit Pizza

This is a combination of two things you love: dessert and pizza.

Prep Time and Cooking Time: 30 minutes | Serves: 12

Ingredients to Use:

1 cup cream cheese, softened

1 teaspoon lime zest

1 tablespoon sugar

17 oz. refrigerated cookie dough

¼ cup strawberries, sliced

¼ cup kiwi, sliced

Step-by-Step Directions

1. Preheat your toaster oven to 350 degrees F.

2. Select bake setting.

3. In a bowl, mix the cream cheese, lime zest and sugar.

4. Spread cream cheese mixture on top of the cookie dough.

5. Top with the sliced fruits.

6. Cook for 15 minutes.

Serving Suggestion: Top with ice cream.

Tip: Use sugar cookie dough.

Apple Tart

Top your flour tortilla with apple slices and cook in the toaster oven for a simple but satisfying dessert.

Prep Time and Cooking Time: 30 minutes | Serves: 1

Ingredients to Use:

1 tablespoon butter, melted

½ teaspoon ground cinnamon

2 teaspoons brown sugar

½ apple, sliced thinly

1 flour tortilla

Step-by-Step Directions

1. Mix butter, cinnamon and sugar in a bowl.

2. Toss apple slices in the mixture.

3. Top the flour tortilla with the apple slices.

4. Place the tortilla inside the toaster oven.

5. Set it to toast.

6. Cook for 3 minutes.

Serving Suggestion: Drizzle with caramel sauce.

Tip: You can also sprinkle apples with salt before toasting.

Lasagna Toast with Avocado

This is another snack recipe that you'd find hard to say no to.

Prep Time and Cooking Time: 20 minutes | Serves: 2

Ingredients to Use:

2 bread slices

¼ cup mashed avocado

1 cup marinara sauce

2 tablespoons ground beef, cooked

½ cup ricotta cheese

¼ cup mozzarella cheese

Step-by-Step Directions

1. Spread avocado on top of the bread.

2. Top with the marinara sauce and ground beef.

3. Sprinkle with the cheeses.

4. Place inside the toaster oven.

5. Choose toast setting.

6. Cook at 350 degrees F for 10 minutes.

Serving Suggestion: Let cool for 5 minutes before serving.

Tip: Use whole-wheat bread.

Bruschetta

These can be served as snack or appetizer.

Prep Time and Cooking Time: 15 minutes | Serves: 12

Ingredients to Use:

1 French baguette, sliced into 12

Olive oil

12 cherry tomatoes, sliced

¼ cup mozzarella cheese, shredded

1 tablespoon basil leaves, sliced

Salt and pepper to taste

Step-by-Step Directions

1. Preheat your toaster oven to 450 degrees F.
2. Choose toast setting.
3. Brush the bread with oil.
4. Top with the tomatoes, cheese and basil.
5. Season with salt and pepper.
6. Place inside the toaster oven.
7. Toast for 5 minutes.

Serving Suggestion: Garnish with fresh basil.

Tip: You can also use Italian bread for this recipe.

Toasted Garlic Bread

Snacks don't get easier than this.

Prep Time and Cooking Time: 15 minutes | Serves: 10

Ingredients to Use:

5 tablespoons butter

2 teaspoons extra virgin olive oil

3 cloves garlic, minced

1 teaspoon dried oregano

Salt and pepper to taste

10 bread slices

Step-by-Step Directions

1. Combine all the ingredients except bread in a bowl.

2. Brush the bread slices with the mixture.

3. Place inside the toaster oven.

4. Choose toast setting.

5. Toast at 350 degrees F for 5 minutes.

Serving Suggestion: Garnish with chopped parsley.

Tip: You can also top with mozzarella cheese before toasting.

Spicy Almonds

This snack will give you the energy you need for the day.

Prep Time and Cooking Time: 15 minutes | Serves: 4

Ingredients to Use:

4 cups almonds

1 tablespoon olive oil

1 teaspoon chili powder

Salt to taste

Step-by-Step Directions

1. Preheat your toaster oven to 350 degrees F.

2. Set it to toast.

3. Spread the almonds in a baking pan.

4. Drizzle with oil.

5. Sprinkle with chili powder and salt.

6. Toast the almonds for 15 minutes, stirring every 5 minutes.

Serving Suggestion: Let cool before serving or storing.

Tip: Store in an airtight container for up to 3 days.

Ham & Cheese Toast

Simple but filling and delicious—these ham and cheese toast will be a regular snack at your home.

Prep Time and Cooking Time: 10 minutes | Serves: 2

Ingredients to Use:

2 teaspoons butter

4 bread slices

2 ham slices

2 cheese slices

Step-by-Step Directions

1. Spread both sides of bread with butter.

2. Top 2 bread slices with ham and cheese.

3. Top with the other bread slices.

4. Place inside the toaster oven.

5. Choose toast setting.

6. Toast at 350 degrees F for 5 minutes.

Serving Suggestion: Serve with a bowl of fresh fruits.

Tip: Use grass-fed butter.

APPENDIX : RECIPES INDEX

Printed by Libri Plureos GmbH in Hamburg, Germany